Negotiation Techniques to Help Your Family, Your Business and Yourself

True Life Stories Gathered Over 80 Years of Experiences

John R. Kilsheimer, Ph.D.

authorHOUSE®

AuthorHouse™
1663 Liberty Drive
Bloomington, IN 47403
www.authorhouse.com
Phone: 1-800-839-8640

First published by AuthorHouse   11/30/2009

ISBN: 978-1-4490-5498-4 (e)
ISBN: 978-1-4490-5499-1 (sc)

Printed in the United States of America
Bloomington, Indiana

This book is printed on acid-free paper.

This book is dedicated to my wife, Betts, who is recently deceased, and to our six daughters, all of whom are in the teaching profession. My career with four different Fortune 500 companies involved several moves and thus many sacrifices from one and all.

Acknowledgments

I wish to first thank three schools, The College of the Holy Cross, Fordham University, and Syracuse University where I obtained my B.S., M.S., and Ph.D. degrees respectively. These excellent institutions gave me the knowledge and training to pursue a successful career.

I also want to thank several mentors who gave me excellent advice and increased my opportunities for advancement in my chosen profession. These would include: Vincent Newe of Fordham University; Joseph Lambrech of Union Carbide; Richard Neblett of Esso Chemical; and Le Herron of The Scotts Company.

Finally, I would like to thank my daughters who have given me support and encouragement in this endeavor. They have helped correct my many grammatical flaws and/or aided in supplying most of the pictures for this book. I would like to specifically thank my daughter, Kathleen, who typed the entire book from my handwritten manuscript. Lastly, I owe special thanks to my daughter, Mary, who is my editor-in-chief and worked tirelessly with me to clarify all my stories so that the reader could appreciate the full meaning of the truisms at the end of each chapter.

Contents

Preface

I grew up in a family with two brothers and two sisters, and later with my wife we had six daughters. Thus, my introduction to negotiation started at an early age.

After serving in WWII with the amphibious forces, I was allotted almost four years of education under the GI Bill. This allowed me to obtain a M.S. and a Ph.D. degree in organic chemistry. This training permitted me to pursue a career in chemical research and also led to several business assignments in the chemical industry. I had the opportunity to negotiate contracts both to purchase and to sell technology involving more than twenty companies located in the U.S., Europe, and Asia.

I initially worked as a research chemist for the Union Carbide Company from 1950 to 1961. I then joined Mobil Chemical for the period 1961 to 1966 where I had the opportunity to gain experience in middle management. I then had a great opportunity and joined the Esso Chemical research department. In addition to being in charge of a major pesticide research operation, I also had the opportunity for a critical business assignment in Europe. Unfortunately, a few years later, Esso had a change in their business plans, and their pesticide operation came to a close in early 1971. I devised a silent auction system to sell Esso's partially developed pesticide technology and carried this negotiation to a successful conclusion.

In mid-1971 I was asked to join The Scotts Company in Marysville, Ohio as Vice President of Research. The group of scientists I supervised included chemists, engineers, plant breeders, agronomists, and specialists in all the pesticide fields. Scotts sold its products in several European countries as well as in the U.S., and I had the opportunity to travel and carry out negotiations overseas. After about six years, I was promoted to senior vice president with responsibilities for manufacturing, distribution, marketing, sales, as well as research and development.

In 1982 I retired to Florida where my wife and I entered the real estate field for eleven years. By the year 2004, my wife's health had deteriorated to the extent that our traveling days were over.

At the urging of friends, my writing hobby became a career. My first book, *How The Navy and I Survived Each Other During WWII*, was published in 2005. My second book, *Bedtime Stories by Chase*, with words of wisdom from our schnauzer dog was published in 2007.

This present book is to acquaint one and all that every day everyone negotiates in some form or another. It was written to assist teenagers and both college and graduate students as they seek new opportunities and form their life values and goals. It is also beneficial for adults to help them perfect their interpersonal relationships. These true life stories with their lifelong truisms will enable people of all ages to learn the techniques that lead to success in everyday negotiations with their families, their businesses, and themselves.

Lifelong Truisms

1. "Try it, you'll like it."
2. Splitting the difference is a strategy that often works best if the two parties are not too far apart.
3. The key is to win the Big Ones.
4. A simple smile and a frown can make a loud sound.
5. Never hire a spy to break a tie.
   Parents beware of "unbiased" advice.
6. What goes around comes around is true both in business and with family.
   What happens after the negotiation tells one if it was a success or not.
7. Too much talk is a sure loss with the boss.
8. "Better a good decision quickly than the best decision too late."
9. Setting a limit can save a fortune.
10. It is only a fool who loses his cool with family, sports, or business.
11. When the carrot comes first, then the stick doesn't look so ominous.
12. A small protective CLAUSE can often look like SANTA.
13. Yes or no can blow the show.
14. Loyalty is a two-way street.
15. Strategic firepower can overcome great odds.
16. Confidence plus cooperation is hard to beat.
17. Opportunity and imagination sell value.
18. Trust is a must or the negotiation goes bust.
19. Life isn't always fair, so don't expect it to be.
20. Strong overreaction is not the best negotiating tool.
21. An eager person's scent can cost real cents.
22. "If you find yourself in a hole, stop digging."
    When both are right, there is no fight.
23. "A lawyer who represents himself has a fool for a client."
24. Have no fear just keep your calculator near.
25. The right words plus a pat beats a fight on the mat.
26. Words can speak just as loud as actions.
27. Flexibility, determination, persistence and faith are the essentials in negotiating your future.

28. When you take your final walk under the exit sign, never slam the door.
29. "All's well that ends well."
30. With the Great Negotiator, you don't always get what you want but you get what you need.

Chapter One
My Mother's Strategy

My mom

Many people of all ages from small children, young adults, and senior citizens are often prone to resisting change. Have you ever tried to get someone to eat a meat or vegetable that they have never had before? It takes a good salesman to get them to take the first bite. In one case my mother suggested that my brother Jim and I should give up our summer vacation mornings for six weeks to go to band camp. We would learn to play instruments so that we could be involved in our public school band the following fall. The band included students mainly from the third to the eighth grades. My mother made it sound like a great opportunity.

As soon as we said that we would try it for a week or two, she brought out a trumpet and a saxophone which she had already bought at a local store. We then realized that she was serious and wanted us to like it. There would probably be little chance to quit after a week or two. As it turned out, we both enjoyed the experience and played in the band for several years.

Now….can it work in business?

I tried my mother's strategy in a business situation. I was hired to head the research operation of The Scotts Company located in Marysville, Ohio, a small midwestern town. Its business dealt exclusively with the lawn, garden, and professional turf markets. This company manufactured many slow-release fertilizers and fertilizer-pesticide combinations. The company was a dominant factor in the home lawn business in the U.S. and parts of Europe. The research department of about one hundred was staffed with professionals in all the major fields such as chemistry, agronomy, entomology (insects), plant pathology (fungi) etc. Approximately 10% of the division was involved in the chemistry of developing a new pesticide. At that time they had few good leads and the costs of obtaining clearance from the Environmental Protection Agency (EPA) for a new product had escalated into millions of dollars. All the basic pesticides that were used in the fertilizer-pesticide combinations in the present line were obtained by arrangements with basic manufacturers. There appeared to be little incentive to try and compete in that area and our need for a new pesticide was quite limited. With the backing of the president of the company, I made the decision to stop new pesticide research.

Some of the chemists in that group had been with the company for several years, while others were short-timers. I met with the group and told them that we were dissolving their part of the division, and all those who wanted to make a career in chemical research should seek employment with a basic manufacturer. We would continue their service with us for a few months while they relocated.

However, there were some who were an integral part of the local community and had several years with the company. I told the group that we had a limited number of important positions that could be offered, but these positions would have very different goals. They would probably never have the opportunity to have a patent with their name on it. If they wanted to stay with the company I said, "Why not try to adapt to a different type of position. If you work hard, I believe you will like it and can make a significant contribution to the company."

Several of the chemists decided to leave and continue their careers in the field for which they had been trained. A few stayed and to a man, they adapted and were glad they had made this decision. One Ph.D. chemist became the safety officer for the company and helped us in many ways to better adapt to new regulations and thus improved our overall safety record. Another Ph.D. chemist significantly improved our quality-control operation and lowered our consumer complaint costs.

This is a great example of the success of my mother's strategy – **"Try it, you'll like it."**

Chapter Two
One of My Early Negotiations

After attending the summer band camp, my mother next arranged for me to take private lessons with a local man who ran a musical instrument store. It was in a second story walk-up on the main street, Fourth Avenue, in Mount Vernon, New York. He was a very easygoing man and a great teacher. After a few years, I became fairly proficient and became first sax in the school band. My teacher suggested that it was now time to obtain a brand new instrument that would have a much improved tone quality. He offered to give me a $25 credit for the used instrument that my mother had bought. This credit would go towards the purchase of a new King saxophone so that the total cost to me for the new instrument would be $100. He let me try it and I could tell right away that it was special.

I had some money in my bank account, but had other plans for it. I decided on an interesting strategy which I had never tried before. I first discussed the financial situation with my mother since she had been the one that had initiated my musical endeavors. I proposed that if she would pay for half of the cost of the new saxophone, I would *arrange* for the other half. She seemed delighted and quickly said yes. Later that evening after my father was alone in the living room, I went in and presented the same *arrangement* to him. He would pay half and I would *arrange* for the rest. He asked about all the details including what store I was dealing with and the quality and price of the new instrument. He finally agreed and we shook hands on it. I thought we had a "done deal."

That night I went to bed with the feeling that obtaining one-half of the money from my mother and the other half from my father was a pretty neat negotiation. However, that night when my parents went to bed, the topic of the new saxophone must have come up in conversation. This led to a loud discussion at breakfast the next morning and my carefully crafted negotiation fell apart. There was no further discussion of a new saxophone for several days. Finally one night my father said, "If you still want the new instrument, your mother and I will split the difference with you. We will pay $50 and you pay $50." I couldn't hide my smile and quickly agreed. I discovered that it is not a good idea to be too clever especially if you will be working with the other party again.

Splitting the difference is a strategy that often works best if the two parties are not too far apart.

Chapter Three
When One Is More Than Many

There were five children in our family so birthdays and other gift-giving occasions were quite frequent. When I was nine years old and approaching my 10th birthday, it was my time to make up a wish list. In the past my brothers and I would make up a long list and hope for the best, knowing that we wouldn't get everything we desired. I wanted a new, large 28-inch wheel bicycle in the worst way. I also knew that it was probably more expensive than several small toys and games. Nevertheless, I let my parents know how much it meant to me, and it could count for both my birthday and other holiday gifts all wrapped into one. On the morning of September 21, 1933 as I awoke, standing at the foot of my bed was a new, blue 28-inch wheel bicycle. That was the greatest and most memorable birthday of my life, and even today I remember it with emotion. That bicycle was my main mode of transportation until I went off to college in 1941.

I learned that in any negotiation it isn't the number of items under discussion that you prevail -

The key is to win the Big Ones.

Chapter Four
How to Respond to a Mistake

I had just finished grade school and was ready for middle school and felt like I was ready for anything. In the past my mother had always gone shopping with me when I needed new clothes. I wanted a new pair of shoes and told my mother to just give me the right amount of money, and I would take the bus to the Tom McCann shoe store by myself. She said okay and gave me ten dollars as there was a big sale being advertised in the local *Daily Argus* newspaper.

When I arrived at the store and saw the big display of shoes, my eyes were immediately drawn to a handsome pair. There was no doubt in my mind that they were "my shoes," and within ten minutes I walked out of that store feeling ten feet tall with my new, brown suede shoes in a handsome box. When I arrived home, my mom asked to see my purchase, but I said let me put them on first and I'll show them to the whole family. When I walked into the living room with my wonderful new purchase, my older brother and sister just started to laugh. My mother frowned at first then just smiled. She asked if I was going to wear them to school. The following Monday I wore them to class and created quite a commotion.

The elegant soft suede with raised embroidered stitching looked quite different from the brown and white saddle shoes worn by most of the students. I was asked if I was going to buy a "zoot suit" or a tux and join a touring blues band. I found that what looked cool was not really the best purchase. I then only wore them on occasions when they would attract the least attention.

My mother never chastised me, but her frown followed by a smile then silence spoke volumes. The next time I needed clothes, she allowed me to shop by myself knowing well that a lesson had been learned.

A simple smile and a frown can make a loud sound.

Chapter Five
Arbitration

When two parties disagree, they often seek a third party to settle the dispute. This can help reach a solution if handled correctly. It usually depends on whether the third party has a bias towards one side or the other. Therefore, great care should be taken when you choose to seek the advice of a third party in any negotiation.

In 1962 I was involved in a situation in Westfield, New Jersey. A group of individuals called the Pool Membership Committee received a permit to build a membership-only swimming pool complex. At that time there was no local public pool available. The city council gave their approval with one caveat- 60% of the membership had to be Westfield residents. A builder was chosen who had the rights to a large tract of desirable land which fit the group's requirements. The pool complex would use part of the land and the builder was free to use the rest as he saw fit. The builder obtained financing and work started immediately so that the pool would be ready for use the following summer. The pool was named Nomahegan, and the group started selling memberships for $300 per family. By late spring it became clear that a large number of members would have to come from outside the city in order to obtain adequate financing. Approximately 60% of the memberships had been sold to non-Westfield residents. The city objected and would not give a certificate of occupancy as the pool would be in violation of a city ordinance which required majority ownership by city residents.

The builder knew that the Pool Membership Committee was in trouble and could violate the timing of taking ownership in their contract with him. He claimed his bank note was due, threatened foreclosure, and said he would take ownership of the pool. The Pool Membership Committee hired an attorney to help them in their dispute with the city and also formed a select group of local citizens to handle the negotiations for them. The people in the group were all interested in the pool, frequently attended city council meetings, and were asked to negotiate a change in the position of the city council. At about the eleventh hour the select group met with the city council and were told it would take three readings, one week apart, to change an ordinance and so it would take almost a month to get the permission the Pool Membership Committee required. There were no other possibilities under the law. The builder said the permit and contract would be in default if the group did not comply within one week. The attorney, whom the Pool Membership Committee hired, met with the select group of which I was a member and told us the builder was adamant in his position and we had but one option and that was to demand the city grant the certificate of occupancy immediately. He told us not to agree to any delay or other procedures.

The group then met in private and after considering all options, we agreed to a plan of action. We met with the city council and let them know how important the pool was for the city as there were no other pools available. We asked them to promise to quickly change the ordinance which limited ownership to mainly city residents. We also agreed that it would take three weeks for the necessary posting of the change. We felt several of the city council appeared favorable to our plea even though it was obvious a few members were against changing the ordinance under pressure.

The select group told the membership committee of our tentative agreement with the city which was directly against the advice of the attorney they had hired. The membership committee then called a number of influential citizens and asked them to contact their council members and also to put pressure on the builder through the local newspaper to delay his legal action. The ordinance was changed in three and one-half weeks and all appeared pleased except the builder and the attorney. I was later told that the services of the attorney, who was hired to give advice to the select group, had previously been utilized by the builder. The builder wanted to control the pool and then build condominiums in the surrounding area.

Nomahegan.net

Nomahegan, an award-winning pool

It is of paramount importance to make sure a third person to help settle a dispute is truly independent and has no bias toward the situation. As a general rule -

Never hire a spy to break a tie.

As a matter of interest, in 2009 the pool complex is still going strong and includes tennis courts and cabañas and has approximately five hundred member families. When it was built in 1962, it was the largest poured concrete pool in the world and was featured in *Life* magazine.

On a personal note, it is of interest that years ago when my wife and I were very concerned about some places our young daughters wanted to go at night, they claimed that a disinterested third party, such as a girlfriend's mother, said it was perfectly safe. Children surely learn at an early age how to negotiate.

Parents beware of "unbiased" advice.

Chapter Six
Ally or Adversary

What do you want to have after the negotiation is over—an ally or an adversary? It is best to make that decision before any discussion starts. If you are an employer and jobs are scarce, it might be tempting to drive a hard bargain during the upcoming contract negotiations. However, workers who believe their employer is both concerned about him or her as well as the bottom line, will usually go the extra mile to make sure the company prospers.

For example, many companies check carefully to see if employees are on time and work a full eight-hour shift. Everyone punches a clock on the way in and out. I worked for a company where the decision had been made many years before that there would be no time clocks. The seven hundred production workers divided into three shifts depended on each other, and the workforce themselves didn't tolerate slackers. A new employee might be surprised at the lack of a time clock but soon would realize it wasn't needed.

Similarly a parent who has a child whose wants exceed their needs has to be careful how dominant he or she wants to appear. My wife and I have six daughters. They each have their own distinct personalities and abilities. Early in their development a family decision was made that although we had limited resources, everyone would have an equal opportunity to obtain a good education including college. This meant that no one could attend an expensive, prestigious northeastern university. All of our daughters graduated from excellent colleges, some from Catholic colleges and some from state universities. They all appreciated the sacrifices that were made to ensure their education.

Our young, happy family looking to the future.

Several years later due to illness the family had significant extra expenses. All six daughters did more than their share financially and physically to help weather the storm.

What goes around comes around is true both in business and with family. What happens after the negotiation tells one if it was a success or not.

Chapter Seven
Is Talk Really Cheap?

One thing I learned the hard way is to be brief. Many people just seem to love to hear themselves talk. In a negotiation excessive talking usually turns out to be a definite negative. You might say something which triggers a new demand from your opposition. Not being precise hurts your credibility with many, and talking too much often infers that your points are not well organized. A dragged out negotiation often fails.

In 1971 I joined The Scotts Company which had just been purchased by the giant conglomerate, ITT, which controlled approximately three hundred companies. Every major company was required to defend in person its next year's business plan. In our first presentation we had our president and vice presidents at one table in a huge room. Opposite us about thirty feet away was a table with close to forty top staff and vice presidents of the parent conglomerate. One chair was vacant. The questioning started around 9:30 am and lasted about two hours. Many of the staff asked long and involved questions. Suddenly the temperature in the room dropped several degrees and in walked Mr. Hal Geneen, the President/CEO. All was quiet for about thirty seconds, and then he questioned us for approximately 25 minutes. The quality, incisiveness, and simplicity of his questions were something that few of us had faced before. As Vice President of Research it was soon my turn. His first question dealt with whether our company could make the claim in our advertising that our fertilizer made a person's lawn greener than the less expensive fertilizer of our competitors. I had been told in advance that short answers were preferred and that "Yes," "No," or "I will quickly find out" were acceptable responses. None of these seemed appropriate. In two sentences I stated that the value of our products was that they were slow release and could be used safely in almost any climate. They would not burn a person's lawn when used in hot weather conditions, but would still give a good response in early spring. We all survived and quickly understood why he was the boss.

Too much talk is a sure loss with the boss.

Chapter Eight
Timeliness

When I first joined The Scotts Company, I found that most of my directors, who were in charge of the different groups, had their offices in a row adjacent to mine. Each director had his secretary with her desk directly in front of his office in the narrow passageway. The secretaries got along very well and so the crowded and less private arrangement was tolerated by everyone. It was supposed to be a "temporary" situation. I had one position to fill and that was a director to seek new opportunities for our company. Once that position was filled, the new director hired a secretary and everything went well for several weeks. He took a short business trip to explore some leads. He then had to go on an extended trip to Japan to explore a possible expansion of our program. His new secretary started to come in a few minutes late each morning and then extended it to an hour late one morning. I talked with her about our work rules with little success. It turned out that she had a night job as a dancer. After another week when she came in an hour or more late on two occasions, I let her know privately that if it occurred again, I would have to terminate her employment. I really didn't want to take action before her immediate supervisor returned. However, the following week she was late again, and at closing time I talked with her after all the other secretaries had left. I arranged for her to get two weeks paid notice but not to return to work.

I was relatively new with Scotts and was afraid the other secretaries might not appreciate one of their own being let go especially when her immediate supervisor was not available. The following morning I met with all the secretaries in our area and let them know of the dismissal. I thought they might be a little upset. Wow, they were very upset. First one, then another, let me know of her feelings. How could I let a new person get away with being late so often when they all had been on time every day for years? They were not upset about her dismissal, but only that it had taken me so long to act! I learned a good lesson. Honest, hard workers don't want a slacker to get special treatment. To them that is definitely not acceptable.

It is good to thoroughly think through all major aspects of a difficult situation, but it is wise to announce your decision in a timely fashion. To quote an axiom from Hal Geneen, a former CEO of the ITT company -

"Better a good decision quickly, than the best decision too late."

Chapter Nine
Negotiating to a Limit

How many times have most of us gone to a store to buy one or two items and left with an armful. Overspending is a hard habit to break and having a credit card handy is no help at all. Setting a limit on how much you will spend is one of the most valuable lessons you can learn to help stay happy and live within your means.

It doesn't matter whether you are going to a grocery store, buying a home, or going on a vacation; if you stay within your prearranged limit, you will almost always come home with a smile and know that you have "done good." That tempting, scrumptious-looking dessert is just a faint memory, and you don't need those calories anyway.

In buying a home or other major purchase there are two separate but closely related limits which are of crucial importance. These are the initial down payment and the maintenance costs.

A friend I knew had a son and with his young family was moving into her southern city from up north. She felt that he was a super achiever and would be a big success. His mother was knowledgeable in real estate and felt she could help him get located in a very nice area. He purchased a large home on an extensive, beautiful wooded lot that also contained a detached garage with living quarters above it. Everything was first class and special. However, the size of the home and the price tag were substantial and above the needs of a small, young family. His mother was quite a negotiator and told me how she had worked "the deal." Since the bank loan was not sufficient, she arranged for the seller to hold a second mortgage on the home. This allowed her son to take possession with only a modest down payment.

Everything looked idyllic for a short period of time as he had come south with some savings from his previous position. However, it became obvious the monthly payments on the two mortgages along with taxes and upkeep were more than the young family could handle. In order to try and solve the problem, the husband wanted his homemaker wife to get a job to help out with their expenses. She felt that keeping up their very large home *was* a full-time job. If she took on an outside position, then her husband would have to take a much bigger role with the housekeeping chores. It was not too long a time before the pressure and strife brought an end not only to the ownership of the home but also to their marriage.

This reminded me of negotiating to the wrong limit. The limit was established as a modest down payment rather than the limit to what they could well afford in monthly payments. In the real estate market of today a large number of homes are being foreclosed as the owners just do not have the funds to meet their new monthly payments. Negotiating only to a down payment limit without fully considering your limits on present and foreseeable future monthly increased costs for mortgage, taxes, utilities, and maintenance is a sure road to disaster.

In a business situation I was forced to utilize the limit principle. In the early 1970s, I joined The Scotts Company in Ohio as Vice President of Research. I found the research department was fragmented and housed in several locations. Part of the organization was actually in a small house, another part was inside a production factory, and yet another was in an office building miles away. Scotts was part of a major conglomerate, and our president made application to the parent company, ITT, to allow us to build a central research building where all the groups could better coordinate their activities. Permission was granted and the sum of one million dollars was allocated to the project. After being firmly informed that not one dollar overrun was acceptable, I was given the opportunity to take charge of the project. Our company's general counsel, John, was the most flexible attorney I had ever met. He always said, "Tell me what you want to accomplish, and I will find a legal way." After reviewing a few contracts from local architects, it was decided that none of them fit our requirements. John then drew up a contract that matched our goal. The going rate for the architectural design and follow-through work was about 8%. Our contract specified that the architect's fee was fixed at 8% of our one million dollar allotment. It was further stipulated that when the approved design was let out for construction, a bona fide bid acceptable to us could not exceed one million dollars minus the $80, 000 architectural fee. If no acceptable bid was received, then the architect had to redesign the building to fit our needs at no extra cost. If an acceptable bid was received at a lower cost figure, the architect still received his full fixed fee of $80,000.

Scotts photo

Scotts Research – Marysville, Ohio

In 1974 a contract was signed with a top quality architectural firm and the plan was put into action. This firm worked with each of my directors who had charge of a research area, and each director had to approve the plan for his part of the building. The architect took great pains and negotiated with each director to ensure that his area was functional but not overdesigned. We received four bids from construction companies. Two of the bids were slightly under our top figure while two were considerably higher. We accepted one of the lower bids and the selected construction company performed up to the architect's specifications. My contribution dealt mainly with the entrance lobby with its wood-burning native stone fireplace and warm décor. Our president made sure that most visiting dignitaries had the pleasure of a grand tour. All of our associates (employees) as well as our parent company were well-satisfied with what had been accomplished, and the building is still a showplace today more than 25 years later.

This is proof that negotiating to a limit can result in a high quality, multifunctional facility.

On a personal note, having six daughters and wanting them all to have an equal opportunity to attend college, my wife and I planned to set limits. We lived in New Jersey when our oldest daughter, Joan, was a senior in high school. She had outstanding test scores and wanted to attended Vassar or Mount Holyoke or a similarly rated university in the Northeast. When we examined the total cost, we knew it was prohibitive for us and not possible. We were considered a middle income family. At that time this meant that we made too much to qualify for significant scholarship help and too little to afford some universities. We countered to our daughter by suggesting that she attend the New Jersey State College of Douglas, which was the women's equivalent of Rutgers University. The cost at that time was approximately $2,000 per year. This did not meet with Joan's desires, so we told her to keep on searching for another college. A friend from high school was making plans to attend Fordham University in New York. Joan researched this situation and the cost would be approximately $3,500 per year and loans were available. My wife and I agreed to cover $2,000 of the cost, and she would be responsible for a $1,500 loan per year. Joan was interested but decided to continue her search.

She finally located a midwestern school where the cost would be just slightly over our limit, but because of her test scores they would grant her a small four-year scholarship. The negotiation was successful. She attended the University of Dayton and not only graduated with highest honors, but also met her future husband there. They currently reside in Florida, and she is now teaching finance at a technical university.

Setting a limit can save a fortune.

Chapter Ten
Anger

Most parents love to watch their children participate in sporting events such as baseball or football. If an umpire calls something even slightly in question against their child, a few parents act like their world is coming apart at the seams. The umpire seldom changes his decision, and the people around the angry parent wish that either they or the aroused parent were somewhere else.

Having six daughters, I managed many girls' softball teams in a city league in New Jersey where we lived for ten years. I witnessed all types of behavior from parents who were managers, base coaches or simply fans in the stands. Almost everyone has an opinion on every close play, but in a critical game some parents' feelings are close to fever pitch. First comes shouting, then off with the hat or cap, and sometimes a leap from the wooden stands to the ground and a confrontation with the offending official. Not many on-field decisions get changed, and I have heard some good officials after a close game say that they don't pay enough to put up with this. The following year they spend their free time elsewhere.

In a business situation, I once received a very irritating phone call from a middle manager of a major agricultural company. The company he represented had invented a new pesticide that was effective in preventing insect damage to many important crops. They had also tested it in a preliminary way on turf. At that time I was working for The Scotts Company which was in the home lawn and garden business, and we had tested it on turf plots in several areas and found it quite effective. Our development director, Jim, contacted them and reached an agreement that we would share data. Each company could apply to the EPA for a permit to sell a formulation for lawn use. Since home lawns were our major business, we organized all available test results and vigorously pursued government approval.

The other company was looking at the larger agricultural market and home lawn use was not a priority for them. As a result, our EPA petition was approved for the use of their chemical in our formulation on home lawns in time for the upcoming spring market. Their turf petition had not yet received approval as they had concentrated their efforts elsewhere. The fact that we could market their product on turf and they could not bothered some of their executives, and a manager was instructed to call me. He insulted our company and me in very *descriptive* language for several minutes. It was probably the most irritating phone call I had ever received. I told him that we had an agreement on this product with his company, and we would handle the product with great care. Furthermore, we were going ahead with our spring marketing plan.

I knew the gentleman who was berating me and asked him why he was making such accusations against our company and me. He finally calmed down and told me that they were embarrassed that we would be selling their product for home use a full season before they could get approval. It was his job to try and make me so upset with their company that I would cancel the agreement. He failed in his attempt and then apologized to me.

It is only a fool who loses his cool with family, sports, or business.

Chapter Eleven
The Importance of Emphasizing Gains

In almost all of my negotiations emphasizing what the other side has to gain has been a powerful tool in accomplishing my goal. When a youngster asks for money to buy an object which his/her heart and mind desires, it often presents a challenge. Many times it is not the money which raises the parent's objection. Rather, it is something that the parent believes is not appropriate for a child at that age or it could be harmful. When the cost is not the problem, then the resolution requires great tact.

The parents can give the reason for their objection but follow that up with a suggestion for something both appealing and more appropriate and which might even cost a little more. A suggestion of a shopping trip together reinforces the parents' position.

In a business situation overseas, the philosophy of emphasizing one's gain came into play in a very strategic negotiation between The Scotts Company and Steinach, a German seed company. Steinach had a good seed breeding program and had developed an improved perennial rye grass named Loretta. Another German company, Wolfe, which worked with our company, Scotts, on sales in Europe had brought this new grass to our attention. Our head of development, Jim, and I had witnessed the German seed trials and were convinced it would do well in the United States and fill a void in our company's seed line. We had met with the Steinach group for over a year both at their headquarters in Bavaria and in the U.S. Our company president requested that our liaison man in Germany, who had an excellent seed background and also spoke fluent German, should handle the negotiations. I would be available but behind the scene. I was in Holland at the time on business so the negotiations were to be held at a hotel in Amsterdam. Our liaison man, Harold, knew that to develop the product in America would take considerable effort and expense so we would require the exclusive growing and sales rights in the United States. Harold met with me and we discussed royalty amounts and other pertinent questions. He decided that he wanted to handle the negotiations by himself and would do it in German. The gentleman representing Steinach spoke some English and had a German lawyer with him who was also fluent in English. Harold met with the Steinach group around five o'clock in the afternoon, and it was hoped the deal would be consummated in time so all of us could have dinner together to celebrate. Around six-thirty in the evening Harold came up to our room and said the whole deal was off as they would not give us exclusive rights in the United States.

I asked Harold if he would mind if I met with their negotiator, Mr. Grundler, whom I had met several times before, to see if I could make some headway. Harold agreed. Jim, my director of development, who also knew Mr. Grundler accompanied me, and we met privately with Mr. Grundler and his attorney. Since they had two people, I wanted us to have two, also.

We started the negotiations around seven o'clock. I wanted to emphasize the positives in the arrangement before tackling our sales exclusive requirement. I let them know how important the Loretta seed product would be to our company and reminded Mr. Grundler of our large seed development group in Oregon and the fact that we were the largest seed company in sales in the United States. We believed that our box seed line which handled improved varieties had sales greater than the next five seed companies combined. I mentioned what royalty income his company could expect once we were in full production. I suggested that they could do much better with us rather than trying to work with a large number of companies that did not have the development capability or the advertising budget that our company possessed. I paused for a few minutes to let the "carrot" sink in. Mr. Grundler and his attorney spoke together in German and then renewed the negotiations. They let us know that they had spent considerable time and money developing their seed line and had never given exclusivity to anyone. I then suggested that a change in their previous position might be to their advantage in this one case in the U.S. I pointed out that it would be very difficult for them to make any significant penetration in the U.S. market by themselves. I thanked them for their time and started to get up from the table. The German lawyer protested and said, "Please wait." He conferred again in German with Mr. Grundler and they started again to discuss with us other aspects of the contract. This went on for three hours. When it was finally obvious that we agreed on all points but one, they again went back to claim that they never gave exclusivity to anyone. I stated, "That was too bad as we would make a good partner for them" and I started to leave again. This time Mr. Grundler said," Please wait." He then agreed to our exclusivity in the U.S.

At ten-thirty just before the hotel closed their dining room, the entire two parties enjoyed a good but overcooked dinner.

Our company sold Loretta seed for over ten years and both companies profited handsomely.

In certain negotiations when there is nothing to lose but everything to gain, playing all your aces up front is necessary.

When the carrot comes first, then the stick doesn't look so ominous.

Chapter Twelve
The One Last "Gimmie"

When one is almost ready to finish a negotiation and believes the other party feels good about what has been accomplished, it is time to consider obtaining one last, apparently small but important concession. This has been accomplished often by many negotiators and should not be overlooked. However, it is of paramount importance that one does nothing to upset all that has been previously accomplished. This final action requires a great sense of timing as well as understanding the motives of the other party. A good example follows.

I was working for The Scotts Company, a lawn and garden firm, whose entire line of products were granular. All the lawn products were applied utilizing a very accurate metal spreader that had settings appropriate for each product. The company had recently developed many new fertilizers for plants and shrubs. However, for the most part it did not have products to prevent damage by insects and fungi which are normally applied in liquid form.

Two professors from a major university in Florida contacted us concerning a new liquid application system they had invented. They were currently seeking patent protection. At that time we were unaware of any liquid system that had the accuracy we required. We obtained a preliminary agreement to examine in detail their applicator and to ascertain our interest in a possible license. Our engineers found that the system was simple to operate, showed great promise, but needed a little further work to enable better accuracy. The two professors and our engineering group were in agreement on the modifications.

It was now time to obtain a binding agreement to protect their invention and give us the manufacturing and marketing rights that our company required. The relationship between the two parties was amicable and the proposition we offered was acceptable to them with few modifications. For exclusive rights to their applicator and any improvements we jointly made, Scotts would pay minimum royalties for a short period of time. After that our company would pay a royalty for each applicator sold with a significant minimum royalty guarantee. They were very pleased with the minimum royalty and the possibility of even higher income.

I decided to suggest one additional "gimmie" clause. If our total royalty payments reached a significant figure, our company could choose in the future to pay royalty only on the number of units sold and not be bound by a minimum royalty guarantee. In that event, our company for the future would have only a nonexclusive license, and the two inventors would be free to market their product through other companies as well as through ours. They felt this was fair and were glad to lock in the initial minimum royalty guarantee.

About two years later the President/CEO of our company chose to retire and the incoming president said he was abolishing my senior management position. I accepted an early retirement buyout. My wife and I retired to Florida and together went into the real estate business.

After a period of time one of the two university professors came to visit and solicit my help. He wanted me to negotiate with my former company on their behalf. The Scotts Company had opted to exercise the "gimmie" clause and not be obligated to pay minimum royalties but only pay on the actual number of units sold which was not very large. The two professors had a possible new client who wanted exclusivity on the apparatus. The professors wanted to get the "gimmie" clause removed from the contract and be able to offer exclusive rights to the new client. I suggested that they should decide how much they were willing to pay my former company to give up their rights, and that a negotiator, other than me, would have a better chance to succeed with the new president.

This is just one example of how a last second "gimmie" clause can have a profound effect on a negotiated contract.

A small protective CLAUSE can often look like SANTA.

Chapter Thirteen
Two "Bad" Words

There are two words which I try to avoid or at least use very seldom in any negotiation. The first often gives something away without obtaining anything in return. The second is a turn-off and tends to make the other side defensive and sets a bad tone for further discussion.

As examples, how many of us have faced one or more of the following questions:

1) Dad, can I borrow the car this afternoon?
2) Do I really have to finish all my food?
3) Is there going to be a layoff at our company?
4) Will I get a raise this year on my anniversary?
5) Don't you think our proposal is reasonable?

An answer of yes or no to any of these typical questions can be troublesome.

Question 1 - If you don't want them to have the car, rather than say "no," give a reason such as you plan on using it yourself or someone else has an urgent trip to make. It is hard to argue too much with these types of responses. Whereas an answer of "no" to the request for the car would probably just lead to further unwanted discussions. If you have no objection to the borrowing of the car, then don't just say "yes." The use of the car is an asset and you could easily obtain a favor, such as picking up a shirt from the cleaners or picking up a few items at the grocery store on the way home. A young person's desire for a car is usually strong enough to accept a few conditions. At least for safety's sake and peace of mind find out where they plan to go, and what time you should expect them to be home.

Question 2 - When I was a youngster, the noon meal on Saturday was always beans and franks. I loved the franks, but not the dreaded beans. My father used to do all the serving and always insisted that we waste nothing as people were starving in China. The dreaded "yes" from my father to my question about having to finish all my food always led to a confrontation. This bothered my mother as well as me. She finally came up with a solution by having the food put on serving platters and insisted that we were all old enough to serve ourselves as the food was passed around the table. I would take a miniscule amount of beans to satisfy that we were not allowed to just pick and choose what we wanted. I disguised the taste of my five beans with a fork full of sauerkraut. My mother was always great at negotiating.

Question 3 - A layoff is always a worry in any cyclical industry and especially so in slow times. As a supervisor you want to keep morale and productivity high, so you don't want workers to be "on edge." If you say "yes" to any inquiry about any possible future layoff, the word will quickly pass around and productivity will take a nosedive. If you say "no" and it happens, even several months in the future, your workers will remember that you said "no" and their trust in you will be damaged. Unless a shutdown is imminent, it is best to indicate that you have not heard of any scheduled layoffs, and the company values the work ethic of all its employees and appreciates their contributions to the success of the company.

Question 4 - As to getting a raise, this sounds like Dagwood in the Blondie comic strip where the only time the boss said "yes" was on the first day of April. Unless you are the senior person who can absolutely make it happen, the answer can never be "yes." If the situation looks promising then you can mention that everyone will be reviewed carefully prior to their anniversary date. If the person is a marginal employee, then it is better to suggest that they try to improve their productivity and increase their value to the company.

Question 5 - In most negotiations the initial proposal by the other party is usually quite favorable to themselves. No matter how preposterous an initial proposal might seem, I would find it difficult to give a blanket "no." I would rather let them know that our company has a proposal which we believe is fair to both sides and that all points of view will be given full consideration. When the differences are significant, the first meeting of the two parties should be as brief as possible. Bad vibes can endanger success and a cooling off period is generally beneficial. The best approach is to seek areas where the differences are small and try to get a few early positive results. It is better to build on small successes then go "hammer and tongs" on the more divisive issues. In any difficult situation you need to plan on spending many hours. Always be prepared to have a back-up proposal but don't ever indicate early that one exists. However, even if their proposal is reasonable, do not accept it initially but have discussions and try to get a last minute "gimmie" clause (see previous chapter).

Yes or no can blow the show.

Chapter Fourteen
Loyalty

Loyalty can be defined as a faithful allegiance to a person or a cause. Unfortunately, loyalty is sometimes lacking in big business, and the result is often disruptive to the work environment.

After working for eleven years for my first employer, Union Carbide, I had the opportunity of joining a new chemical division being formed by the Mobil Oil Company. Dr. Burt Miles was hired to start a new chemical research department. He then hired five managers who would be responsible for engineering, general chemicals, polymer development, analytical development, and agricultural pesticide research. I was given responsibility to initiate the pesticide program. A laboratory to house the department was still under construction in Metuchen, New Jersey, so our initial duties were to develop new programs and to assist in recruiting. For five years I had the responsibility of recruiting at several universities, including Princeton and Yale, and conducted on-site interviews of candidates recruited by the other managers. The research department grew rapidly and progress was evident in many of the programs.

One day Al, an old colleague of mine from Fordham University, came to the research laboratory and by chance I met him in the lobby. I quickly found out that he had been hired as Mobil Chemical's new Vice President of Research. The atmosphere around our research department soon changed. Dr. Miles who had hired all of the initial five managers was soon terminated. Al brought in his own Director of Research, a man he knew from Cornell University. The atmosphere had no sooner quieted down before the manager of general chemicals suddenly left the company. I was then named manager of organic chemical research and given a sizeable raise. My responsibilities included several areas including industrial chemicals as well as research on new pesticides.

About one year later one of the men on Al's staff in New York informed our director that he was negotiating a license for a new oxidation catalyst. We were told that he could obtain a very favorable contract. I had recently promoted one of my more experienced chemists to direct our industrial chemicals program, and he was assigned to carry out a thorough evaluation of the catalyst. He found it not equal to others already on the market, and in his verbal presentation to a meeting of both local and New York management, he went so far as to mention that it would probably not be a valuable asset to purchase.

A few weeks later as I was reporting back from vacation, the vice president met me at the front door of the research building and told me he wanted the man in charge of industrial chemicals fired that day. I protested and let Al know how capable the man was and that he had recently been promoted for all the excellent work he had accomplished. The vice president would not negotiate a reprieve. In my vacation absence the director of research and the vice president had made the decision that the man was no longer needed, and he was terminated that day.

Two years later I was in a somewhat similar situation. Our research group had discovered a new insecticide. It had a broad spectrum of activity both on resistant household pests and on insects affecting many high cash crops. It also had passed stringent safety tests on both rabbits and mice. A major meeting was held in our New York office as I had recommended that the product be elevated to a full scale market evaluation. Earlier that week, Roger, who had directed the field trials, assured me he was going to give a highly favorable report on the market for the product. However, when the time came to give his report in front of the vice president and his staff, he decided to play it safe. He gave a much lower sales target than I had been projecting, but then hedged it by saying that continued evaluation could lead to a higher figure. His report was both confusing and disappointing.

The vice president and our director of research evidently got together after that meeting. I went back to our laboratory in Metuchen and shortly before leaving work, I was told by the director that I was being demoted and part of my staff would no longer be reporting to me. In addition, I was told that I should not expect any future raises.

I felt that the director of research had not stood up for me and the vice president should have had more faith in my judgment. My present situation seemed somewhat similar to the treatment afforded my former head of industrial chemicals. I was quite sure the sales target given at the New York meeting was not accurate. After one month of numerous phone calls to the vice president, I finally convinced him to hire an independent agricultural consultant to reassess the market potential. After a six-week study the consultant not only verified my market projection but gave a slightly higher figure. I was vindicated but was not satisfied with the status quo as nothing had changed with respect to my responsibilities.

After much thought and soul-searching discussions with my wife, I decided to look for another position. I was quickly offered an opportunity with another company and promptly tendered my resignation. Surprisingly, within one day I was offered a possible raise and the return of all my responsibilities if I would stay with Mobil Chemical. I believed that the lack of loyalty by both the research director and vice president could very possibly reappear in the future. I declined their offer to renegotiate my decision.

Incidentally, within a relatively short period of time, all of the original five managers hired by Dr. Miles who had initiated the research department had left the company.

I learned a very valuable lesson. Loyalty to your boss is only one facet of the negotiation equation. Loyalty to those reporting to you is just as essential.

Loyalty is a two-way street.

Chapter Fifteen
Negotiating With the Boss

In the mid 1960s I was hired by Esso Research to advise on a newly formed agricultural pesticide program. After a few months, I was made director of the program. I answered to Richard, the director in charge of the company's entire agricultural program including pesticides and fertilizers. A significant number of well-trained Ph.D. chemists right out of graduate school had been hired, and they were joined by several experienced chemists and engineers who were already with the company. We had one chemist who could head up the group working on new herbicides and fungicides. However, I felt we needed a person knowledgeable in phosphorus chemistry to head up the insecticide group. The company also had a well-funded, long-range basic research group in which the chemists could work on almost anything they chose. One of these chemists, Al, let us know he would be interested in joining our operation. He had been working in an area of phosphorus chemistry closely related to some commercial insecticides. My boss and I both believed that the fit would be advantageous, and he joined our group. One of the long-term company chemists in an advisory capacity to my boss told us that we would rue the day we brought him on board. However, the match between Al's strong background and our needs seemed important enough to take the risk.

Everything seemed to work well for almost a year. A few of our young Ph.D.'s quickly learned the field and started to come up with new ideas of their own. Our new insecticide leader, Al, had been accepted to give a research paper at a major chemical conference. We were led to believe it was on work he had done while he was in his previous position. After the meeting, a friend of mine from another company called and let me know that he was surprised that we would release information on products that were quite biologically active and were being presented as recent research findings. My friend sent me pictures of all the slides that were presented by Al. To my shock some of the materials on the slides were of compounds that were not yet covered by patents, and should never have been released. They indicated the direction of our research program. This led to a meeting with Al. It was very short and direct. I let him know that he had made a serious error in judgment in releasing information on an active research program. Further, from now on all future material he wanted to publish or present at conferences had to be approved by management. He strongly disagreed with almost everything I said and let me know my position was not acceptable. He felt that he had the right to publish whatever he chose.

After this conversation, our relationship deteriorated. His resentment towards me became obvious to both my boss and the entire group. I let my boss know that I believed that we should replace Al with a new group leader as the situation was very divisive to our whole program. Within two weeks the Vice President of Research invited me to an after-hours meeting in his office. When I arrived, Al was in attendance, and I was told that charges had been brought up against me. The vice president decided that as each grievance was mentioned he would write it on the blackboard in his office. In total there were approximately twenty problem areas cited. Interestingly, one of the earlier claims was that I tried to dictate closely the work the new chemists should pursue; however, claim #20 stated that I did not give enough guidance to the work of the new chemists. The vice president pointed out the apparent discrepancy, and after a short discussion, the formal meeting ended. The vice president knew of my plans to appoint a new group leader, and as he closed the door, he let me know I could not make any changes unless he approved. I then knew that I would have to use an indirect approach. Over the next few weeks, things deteriorated even further. I checked on the vice president's schedule and learned he was going to be away for several days. I decided to initiate my plan of action.

I first had a discussion with my direct supervisor, Richard, and let him know the present situation was detrimental for the entire group. I further asked him who he thought would be a good replacement for Al. Richard suggested Jim, whom Richard had hired two years earlier. He had both a Ph.D. in organic chemistry and a pharmacy degree and had shown great progress in developing new compounds for the insecticide group. I then called the vice president's office and asked to speak with him on an urgent matter. As expected, his secretary told me he would be away for several days. I requested that she put a note on his calendar that I had called. That afternoon I removed Al from his position. The following day my boss, Richard, and I named Jim as the new group leader in charge of insecticides.

I was a little uneasy for the rest of the week waiting for the vice president to return. He never called me on the subject but just requested that Richard have Al report directly to him rather than to me. Within two months my boss ended that arrangement, and Al was transferred back to the long-range research group.

It is to the vice president's credit that he never held this matter against me. The fact that my immediate boss picked the replacement certainly came up in their conversation and proved to be a significant part of my strategy.

As they taught in naval gunnery school -

Strategic firepower can overcome great odds.

Chapter Sixteen
Gain Their Confidence;
Win Their Cooperation

www.faqs.org/faqs

France

One of the more interesting business challenges I have faced was an assignment in the late 1960s to work with the French company, Esso Chemie, which was part of the parent, Esso Company. The New York office felt that my knowledge of the pesticide business might help identify the source of the French company's problems. The profitability of their pesticide division had declined rapidly. I did not speak French and none of their people had ever met me so I knew there would be some initial obstacles to overcome in order to obtain their cooperation. The background of this complex story follows.

Shortly after the end of WWII, Esso Research had discovered the fungicide, Captan. Esso management made the decision not to enter the pesticide business. They licensed Captan to Standard Oil of California for development in the United States and some countries overseas. Esso would benefit by receiving royalties and it cut its expenses by curtailing its research program in the United States. However, Esso retained the marketing rights in France as it was very effective against fungus problems on grapes. Esso Chemical France, known as Esso Chemie, headquartered in Paris had developed a very successful broad agricultural pesticide sales program using Captan as their leading product. They had at least one salesperson in every province in France and the pesticide division was quite profitable for several years. However, by 1968 the profitability had essentially vanished.

In the 1960s Esso had once again started an agricultural research program in Linden, New Jersey. After working in the pesticide field for several years, I joined Esso and took charge of the pesticide research program in 1966. When the profitability of their French pesticide program became acute, I was sent to Paris by the New York office as an "advisor." After arriving in France as the "American from New York," I received a very warm reception from upper management and was asked to take charge of a review of the entire pesticide operation and a possible reorganization of their program. However, my initial reception by key members of the pesticide personnel was rather cool.

One of my first endeavors was to ascertain the cost basis for each of their pesticide formulations. Pierre Dauguet, the head of their Research and Development (R&D) program, had a major influence on their entire pesticide operation and I needed his cooperation. By the end of the third day, he agreed to accompany me to the formulation company that made all the products that Esso Chemie sold. The formulation company was located in Rouen, the famous city where Joan of Arc met her death. Previously I had our Esso formulator in the U.S. develop for me the approximate cost basis for every product Esso Chemie sold. After going through the Rouen plant, I learned that most of their equipment was large volume oriented and was fully depreciated. The equipment was also being used for many other products not related to Esso. It became obvious that Esso Chemie was being overcharged. The plant manager of the formulation company then made the startling statement that they kept two sets of books and admitted that they were overcharging on many Esso products. He agreed to make immediate corrections.

Word passed quickly that I had helped reduce their costs, and doors flew wide-open to almost immediate cooperation by Esso Chemie R&D, sales, and middle management. We then made a detailed analysis of the marketplace and found that the problem centered on the product, Captan. This one product had been responsible for at least 40% of the gross profit of their pesticide operation. The use patent for Captan had expired, and the German company, Bayer, had entered the French market with a low-priced Captan product to gain market share. Esso Chemie had several marketing areas, each with some degree of independence. As a result when the Bayer Captan product came into their area, the Esso Chemie marketing group cut their price and their overall profitability was severely reduced.

Pierre Dauguet, who had accompanied me earlier to Rouen, informed me that he had been testing a new fungicide which the DuPont Company was developing. It was equal to or better than Captan and was just getting approved in France. Due to the dominance of the Esso program in the grape market, DuPont was willing to give Esso Chemie an exclusive position. In a meeting with the R&D and marketing people, I found that each salesperson received a percentage of the sales of each product in his area. Sales management then agreed to drastically reduce the incentive each salesperson received on Captan and gave a generous percentage to each salesperson on the new DuPont fungicide formulation where the markup was significant. The sales force quickly got the message and encouraged their main clients to switch to the new product. The sales force was reorganized and some small agricultural provinces were combined into one territory. This freed up personnel to expedite the introduction of the new product in the more lucrative areas.

Once everyone was on board, it was a win-win situation. The lowering of the cost for each formulation by the company in Rouen resulted in only a modest saving to Esso Chemie. However, it indicated to all the personnel in the pesticide division that I was there to help them. Quickly everyone started to understand that change was in their best interest. Their confidence in me and the new program and their cooperation in adapting to all the changes led to financial success within one year

Confidence plus cooperation is hard to beat.

Chapter Seventeen
Selling Before eBay

Whether it is an interesting gadget, a bicycle in reasonable condition, or a technology no longer wanted by a company, there are a few good points to always consider when one wants to maximize the return. First, make a list of all the unique features of the item in question. While some features might not interest everyone, they might be of great value to someone. Second, identify who or what group of individuals would be most likely to purchase the product, namely the target audience. Third, ascertain the most cost-effective way to bring the item to the attention of the target audience. Fourth, price the product so that people will expect it to have great value and be worth their time, effort, and money to obtain it

Around 1970, Esso, a major Fortune 500 company for which I worked, made the decision to greatly curtail their position in the agricultural chemical marketplace. They had a very heavy investment in fertilizer manufacturing plants which at that time were not very profitable. They also had a limited sales position in the pesticide market (insecticides, herbicides, and fungicides) all outside the United States. Additionally, over the last five years they had developed a well-funded R&D program that had a significant number of promising pesticide chemicals in field trials. The most advanced product was a herbicide which would prevent weeds from developing but was safe to soybean seedlings. This product was about a year away from test marketing and had looked extremely promising in United States Department of Agriculture (USDA) field trials. In other categories such as insecticides, fungicides, etc., there were several promising candidates, but they were not as far along in the development process.

A management decision was made to initiate a withdrawal from the agricultural business and immediately phase out the R&D effort. This was a major blow to the pesticide research team as they had great hope for several of their new products. As head of the pesticide program, I put together a plan on how to sell partially developed technology. The plan divided all of the chemicals into four classes depending on whether they affected insects, weeds, etc. The pesticide technology sale was made known to a large number of companies worldwide. They were informed that we would carry out a silent auction. Any company could make an initial trial bid on any of the four classes, but a nonrefundable down payment of $5,000 per class was required. For the initial deposit they would be given coded samples of the most advanced products in that category so that they could test them in their own laboratories. They were also given the location of all the private and USDA field trials so their representatives could visit the sites and talk with the field investigators. A secrecy agreement was required to ensure that they would not investigate the chemistry of any of the coded samples.

Eighteen companies paid the initial $5,000 payment on each class in which they had an interest. After a time interval of approximately three months, a company could bid on any class for which they had made the initial deposit. This final bid would include not only a significant down payment, but also how much they would spend on a development effort to examine the full potential of the class and what amount of royalty they would pay for any product that went commercial. Our company would be the sole judge on which bids to accept. Once a bid was accepted for each class and the nonrefundable significant down payment received, the company would be given all our information. This would include patent applications, structure-activity correlations, engineering data, etc. The only caveat was that after they received the data, they had a limited time period in which they could back out of the agreement with just the loss of their significant down payment.

After all bids were examined in great detail, winners were declared for each of the four categories. The various companies' bids differed greatly in the amount of their significant down payment. The successful bids ranged from one hundred thousand dollars to five hundred thousand dollars. One of the winning companies eventually backed out and lost their down payment. That class was resold to a bidder who had already purchased another class and knew of the original sale. The total money our company received was a seven-figure number and shortly royalties were received on the most advanced product.

This entire negotiation occupied several months of my time both in its planning and execution. However, I enjoyed every moment of it and our senior management was both surprised and very pleased at the extent of its success. As far as I know this was the first time the sale of partially developed technology had ever been handled in a negotiation in this fashion. Both my immediate boss, Richard, and I were rewarded for our endeavors.

Opportunity and imagination sell value.

Chapter Eighteen
A Key Essential is Trust

In the previous chapter the sale of partially developed technology is outlined. One Japanese company contacted Esso after hearing about the silent auction and the possibility of obtaining a potentially valuable product. However, we learned of their interest when there were only about six to seven weeks left before final bids were due. This put them at a serious disadvantage in the testing and evaluation phase. They were interested in only one of our categories and that involved chemicals to control fungi. We had one compound which in early field trials looked very promising. They had heard of it at a government field station where it was being tested under a code number. They wanted to test it on rice problems in Japan.

On the first day all discussions with the key person from Japan were carried out through an interpreter whom they had brought with them to our laboratory. They asked for several deviations from our auction format. Their requests were reasonable on the surface and my boss, Richard, who was a very amiable man, agreed with their requests. I had to quickly intervene and pointed out that all companies had to play by the same rules. For example, I acknowledged that they had very limited time to test the material, but we had a deadline when all bids had to be received so we could not grant an extension. Other requests were made and although my boss seemed to agree with them, I had to continue to intervene and disagree, thus feeling like the bad guy in all the discussions. But I knew it was necessary.

After two days we finally came to an agreement which recognized all the points in our general contract with all the other companies. As we began the second day, their main negotiator then let us know that he was fluent in English, and in fact we found his English far superior than the translator's. He had been playing coy and wanted to learn the essence of any discussions that were going on between my boss and me.

Interestingly, he let us know that he had been an unsuccessful kamikaze pilot so he had lived to tell the tale. He could speak eloquently, and we learned that he was their company's senior man in the U.S. The agreed upon contract was then sent to Japan for review.

About a week later I received a call from the company and was invited to a victory dinner the following week in Manhattan. They had received the approval to bid on the technology. After a few days my boss never said a word about the dinner, but I couldn't believe he had not been invited. I called a good friend who now worked for the Japanese company, and he told me they were not going to ask my boss as they did not trust him. They said he first smiled and agreed to some of their points, but later changed his mind during the negotiations. I wasn't sure what to do so I said nothing to Richard and went alone to the victory dinner. It was in a first-class Japanese restaurant in New York City.

The next week a meeting was set up in Japan for the signing of the agreement. My boss told me he was going to Japan in my place. He would bring an attorney to help seal the deal and they didn't feel it was necessary to send three people. I was very disappointed to say the least, but there was nothing I could do. I never mentioned the victory dinner to my boss as I didn't know an easy way to explain it. After they returned from Japan, they had no signed agreement, but Richard said they expected it in the mail. It never came. The Japanese did not trust Richard and bringing an attorney whom they had never met did not improve the situation.

Trust is a must or the negotiation goes bust.

Chapter Nineteen
The "Fairness Doctrine"

Sometimes after a negotiation is finished the result is not always perfect. Whether it be an agreement, a contract, or even a law, sometimes it is just not fair to everyone. I worked in New Jersey for five years for a large research organization that treated me very well at all times. There was a local union which represented the hourly laboratory assistants and the union and the company had almost no significant disagreements while I was there. One evening and early the following morning there was a very heavy snowstorm. Many streets were impassable and schools were closed. My home was only a few miles away from the laboratory, and I was able to get to work only a few minutes late. I utilized main roads that had been sufficiently plowed to allow minimum traffic flow. At this time only about one-third of the hourly workers had arrived. By ten o'clock several more workers had come in and by noon approximately two-thirds of the hourly employees had reported for work. Many had horror stories about how they had overcome the weather elements and many snowdrifts.

The next day the "Fairness Doctrine" was in for a shock. The one-third that did not make it to work were mostly long-term associates, and they claimed that they were sick. They all received full pay for the missed day. All those hourly employees who had struggled to make it into work but were late received no pay for every hour they missed. This seemed grossly unfair so I took it up with my supervisor. He quoted the union contract that each person was entitled to a fixed number of sick days and no doctor's note was required for the first day of illness. He further explained that if the company made any exception to the contract, the union could argue that they, too, could make exceptions. This could lead to chaos. The result was that those who had tried hard but were late were punished financially.

In another situation the "Fairness Doctrine" came into play when I was working in Columbus, Ohio. I joined a group called The Saint Vincent de Paul Society. Several of us would visit the main prison every week to meet one-on-one with prisoners who were awaiting trial and could not make bail. The charges against them varied from petty theft to murder. Each prisoner was allowed only one phone call per week, so the requests to us were quite varied. Most of the men were of very modest means and were represented by court-appointed attorneys who had very large caseloads. Too often the first time a prisoner met his attorney was when he was officially brought up on charges. In one case a young man who was well known to us and the police was in deep trouble. He had spent some time in jail because of a few misdemeanors, but we felt he had rehabilitated himself. He was now charged with a serious felony. After a store break-in, the police did a sweep of the entire area, and this young man was picked up a few blocks away from the scene. The police had no other leads so he was charged with the crime. His court-appointed attorney did not have sufficient time to thoroughly work the case, so he met with the assistant district attorney and came up with a possible negotiated solution. If the young man confessed to the break-in, the charge would be reduced to a misdemeanor with a recommendation of a very modest jail sentence. The alternative, if he came to trial, could be a felony conviction with several years of hard time. The court-appointed attorney told us he felt the man was innocent, but there was insufficient time or funds to track down all the details. The plea bargain was accepted and the police could then close the case as solved. Our group felt that the "Fairness Doctrine" was challenged once more. One's past can overshadow one's future.

Life isn't always fair, so don't expect it to be.

Chapter Twenty
Water on the Rocks

While in graduate school at Syracuse University during the Korean War, there were times when student unrest manifested itself in street demonstrations which caused minor damage. At times some of the roads near campus became impassable due to rock throwing and other threats to cars. The police were called and they tried to strong-arm the students into submission. Usually there were brief skirmishes and some students were booked for disorderly conduct. There would be a lull, the police would leave, and then the ruckus would start again. After a few days of periodic unrest, the fire department was called in to help. They immediately connected their hoses to the closest fire hydrants and started to spray the protestors. If they charged the firemen, the spray turned into a strong water force which stopped the unruly students in their tracks. The water pressure would then be reduced to a light spray. It reminded me of the water sprays some urban cities used on hot days to give the kids some summer fun.

Within one day the students grew tired of getting continuously soaked. No one was hurt, the firemen never touched a person, and everything quieted down. As one fireman remarked, "Sugar works better than salt."

Strong overreaction is not the best negotiating tool.

Chapter Twenty-One
Buying a Used Car

Up front, I have to admit that one of the areas I never mastered was negotiating with a used car salesman. I have a good friend, George, who is retired from the used car business. I always refer to him as a used car salesman, but he corrects me and reminds everyone within earshot that he was a used car dealer - he owned the operation. He further claims that he was strictly honest in every transaction. I am always happy to meet one of a kind.

My first experience in buying a car was in 1949. I was in graduate school working on my Ph.D. in chemistry, and my wife had just turned twenty-five and had received a very small stipend from her father's will. It was a week before Easter, and it was the first time we had seen more than one hundred dollars at one time since we were married in 1946 as I had gone back to school after being discharged from the Navy.

We were living in abandoned army barracks that were converted into student living quarters, and it was more than a mile walk to the chemistry building at Syracuse University. We made a list of all the things that we thought were almost necessities - items that we had done without for the last few years. We had no telephone, no baby carriage for our one-year- old daughter, no electric refrigerator, no piping systems to get the kerosene from the 55 gallon drum in the backyard into the pot belly stove in the living room, etc. A car was quite far down the list. My wife, Betts, and I negotiated and agreed that $300 was the maximum we could splurge on a car. This would happen only after items on the earlier "must list" were taken care of first.

My bus ride to downtown Syracuse was filled with hope and excitement. I had not had this amount of money in my pocket since shortly after the day I had said, "I do." We, of course, had no credit cards and lived, as most of the graduate students did, mainly on our monthly stipend from the GI Bill. The first place I stopped had nothing available for less than $500. At the second place there was a 1935 Ford with front and back seats, yellow fog lights, an oscillating fan to cool the driver, and acceptable tires. I asked the salesman how much they were asking for it. He asked me how much I had. I truly believe that when a person gets excited about a car, he must give off a special scent which is readily picked up by an experienced used car salesman. I was allowed to drive the car just around the block, and he soon had my $300. I later realized many of the reasons why the previous owner had traded in the car. These included the radiator which would overheat every time the car went up a steep hill and the mechanical brakes which would overheat and fail if you had to use them too often. Fortunately, the road from the barracks to school was quite level.

Many years later I was in the market for a used car for my oldest daughter to drive to work for her summer job. I went to a car dealer where I had recently bought a new car and was very satisfied. The salesman showed me a used car he claimed was in excellent condition and quoted me a price. In my naivety I asked if that was the best price he could give me. He read me like a book and said it was rock bottom. I paid the full asking price. Years later I learned to bring someone else with me who knew the territory.

The following are lessons that I have learned. It is better not to indicate that one specific car is your favorite, instead ask questions about several. If it is just one car you like because of the make, model, year, etc., the salesman knows you are "his" because that specific car may not be readily available all over town. It could be like a fish that swallowed the hook. He could play you a little and then slowly reel you in. It would be better to discuss the price and specific attributes of several cars. Indicate that you will have to think it over and start to walk away. The salesman then will usually give you his card. Finally, you can make your move by telling him you have only so much money to spend; therefore, you can only go so high on the particular car that you want. After some further discussion, you will probably agree on an intermediate price. However, before the agreement is concluded make sure that you can first have the car checked out at your local repair shop. Also obtain the name of the previous owner to see why he made the trade. In addition, one can often obtain a lower price towards the end of the month when a salesman is trying to make his quota.

There are two other factors which some people use. First, shop at dusk so the salesman can't easily read your excitement and expression when you see that special car of your choice. Second, when there is a breeze keep downwind of the salesman in case it is true that an excited buyer gives off a scent which a good used car salesman can pick up immediately.

An eager person's scent can cost real cents.

Chapter Twenty-Two
Negotiating With a Spouse

There are two main types of spousal negotiations. The first is where there is a major difference in opinion, and the discussion can easily get heated and possibly acrimonious. The best solution is to obtain a truce as quickly as possible. It is of paramount importance to quickly let your spouse know that you understand his/her point of view and that it is reasonable. However, let your spouse know there are conflicting circumstances that also need to be considered. A quick truce is better than a long argument every day of the week. Eventually cooler heads prevail and the question in point usually has to be broken into smaller parts and each item discussed separately. The problem often concerns money and how much and when it should be spent.

As to this type of negotiation, Will Rogers had the best solution - **"If you find yourself in a hole, stop digging."**

The second type of spousal negotiation can most often be solved and have a win-win resolution. This happens frequently when the couple has different priorities, but where the two are not in direct conflict.

For example, on a personal note, my wife and I decided to sell our oceanfront condominium where we had lived for eighteen years. It was to have a major reconstruction program which would take about a year. The big decision was where to move. In our discussion my wife wanted to get away from the beach and the crowds which had been getting larger every year. On the other hand, I was used to living with a water view and a place to fish right outside the door.

Unfortunately our pet schnauzer, Charlie, had died a few years earlier and my wife sorely missed having a pet. He was a great companion and guarded our condo unit and my wife any time he saw me leave with my fishing pole.

After searching awhile for a solution, we found the right compromise. We moved into a gated manufactured home community of seven hundred units. We purchased a three bedroom home, set back from the road and directly on the main channel of the intercoastal waterway. Also, within a month a three-month old miniature schnauzer, we named Chase, joined the family. Things are great in a win-win compromise.

Chase – I love it here!

As to the second type of negotiation -
When both are right, there is no fight.

Chapter Twenty-Three
When In Deep Trouble

Most of us have found ourselves in serious trouble sometime in our life, and there is truly one solution that works best almost all the time. In the first year of my naval career we had about six weeks off from our studies. Along with several of my classmates I had volunteered for a three-week "cruise" at the naval training station in Newport, Rhode Island. One of our officers, Lt. McGoffelin, and two of our chiefs had accompanied us on this summer program. For some reason which I could never identify Chief Schiavoni was antagonistic towards me, and frequently corrected me for any violation he perceived. Several mornings each week he would inspect our barracks, come to my bunk and rip off the sheets and blankets, and yell that it was not made to naval specifications. I would then remake it and he would leave. My only other mishap that I can recall was when I was late reporting to an observation tower and ran into Lt. McGoffelin. The rest of the "cruise" including a trip on a PT boat, a gas mask drill in an active gas chamber, and anti-aircraft machine gun firings all went very well.

When the three weeks were over, I was told that I alone had received enough demerits and had flunked the "cruise." Further, there would be a hearing to decide if I should be dropped from the officer training program. This was a great shock as I never thought the "cruise" could damage my naval career. I had already signed up for four years and going to boot camp was not in my plans. I knew I needed help "big time." I selected a fellow "cruisemate," John Noone, to represent me. He was first in our class, had impeccable credentials, and was well liked by all our superiors. I talked with John about the chief's apparent bias against me, and the fact that I believe almost every demerit was from him. John decided on a completely different approach. He was not going to get into a nitty-gritty argument concerning the bunk episodes. At the hearing he spoke very briefly. He made the point that the "cruise" was voluntary and that less than half of our class had participated. I believe he further stated that in all the exams, I never failed one and thus did not require any re-exams. Therefore, my interest in this naval program was sincere and exceeded that of over half the entire class who chose not to participate in the summer training. After a short recess, I was told that I would remain in the program with just a three-month probation period.

My Navy life   1941-1946

John Noone was the right man, at the right time, with the right ideas to help keep my naval future on track. When in trouble, seek the best individual with good advice to help you. Don't just try to go it alone.

There is an old saying –

"A lawyer who represents himself has a fool for a client."

Chapter Twenty-Four
Negotiations in Silence

Most of us think that a negotiation involves two or more people with different points of view trying to come to an acceptable solution. However, almost every day all of us negotiate with one or more large companies who silently and usually successfully convince us that we are receiving a bargain for our twenty or more nickels. I believe that many might still remember when a nickel was a real important coin. When I was quite young, about once a week my mom would give me a nickel so that I could buy a treat after school on my walk to my saxophone music lesson. There was a nice man with a vending truck who always parked just outside of the schoolyard. Many of us would flock to his truck for a treat. He had the biggest assortment of candy, gum, and other delicious treats and most everything cost a nickel. A Milky Way bar or other tasty bit of chocolate was usually my choice. I would just unwrap the end, take a very small bite, and slowly munch on it all the way to my music lesson. A few years later, however, no matter how slowly I munched, it was all gone while I was still a block or so from my music teacher's store. I realized that even though the outside wrapper looked the same, the candy inside was smaller. A few years later the candy bar got bigger again, but now it cost two nickels.

As I grew older and started to shop, I loved to buy coffee. I would purchase a pound and put it through a machine which ground it up, and the aroma was incredible. In school they had taught us a pound of anything was sixteen ounces. However, in time a "pound" of coffee started to change. Today it is only about eleven or twelve ounces, but the price has not been reduced accordingly.

My wife and I have six children, all girls. When everyone came home for the holidays, it appeared we had to stock up on paper for the bathroom. We had always bought just single rolls which lasted a few days. However, soon we had to go to double rolls. The so-called double rolls did not have twice as many sheets as the old single rolls. I am sure triple rolls are just around the corner. It seems that as everything gets bigger, the amount actually received per dollar gets smaller. We were once taught that if you bought in volume, things would be cheaper. I guess that was true in the good old days. However, history does repeat itself. Have you counted the number of cans in your soft drink carton recently?

Have no fear just keep your calculator near.

Chapter Twenty-Five
Empathy Yes; Sympathy?

When you approach the person with whom you are going to have a negotiation, sometimes it is evident that he (he/she) is not one hundred percent comfortable. There could be personal reasons or lack of experience with the negotiation process. It is best to try to clear the air with some initial small talk. Just asking if he had a chance to watch a recent major sports event might elicit a response as to why he could not watch it because he was occupied with a serious personal matter.

To be successful in the negotiation you want to have your counterpart comfortable that his interests will be carefully considered. The person usually doesn't want sympathy but rather to have someone else understand that things have been difficult. One of the worst things you can do is find out what the problem is and then start to relate how you can sympathize with him as you or a close friend have been through the same thing. The person with whom you are about to negotiate is really not interested in hearing all about your problem at that moment.

While I was working on this story, an example that helps illustrate this point came into play. An out-of-town family member called to see how I was doing. I mentioned that the pastor of our church had gone fishing that morning with a friend, and while moving from one fishing spot to another, the priest fainted and died of a heart attack. This priest, a few months earlier, had said the Mass, given the eulogy, and presided at the graveside burial of my wife. My caller had been there and met him personally. After expressing his surprise and sympathy, he immediately started to recount how a friend of his who was on an automobile journey with her husband never reached her destination. She in turn suddenly passed away. I really did not appreciate hearing all the details of that story right then. I suppose it is natural for people to suddenly remember a trauma story of their own, but it is better kept to another day. This is especially true in a negotiation situation.

For some people showing empathy is natural, but for most of us it takes experience to simply show heartfelt understanding. This is much appreciated by the other person and allows him to get back on point in a reasonably short time.

If you are middle-aged and are dealing with a child, adolescent, or senior citizen, your points of reference on a subject are probably far different than theirs. Special consideration is required in these situations. Patience is a virtue and for some of us, it takes a lot of practice. While watching a rerun of the Andy Griffith show one evening, a great point was made. The young son, Opie, was not earning the grades in school which his dad, Andy, thought were up to his potential. He gave Opie a stern lecture and then made it mandatory that he come straight home from school. Opie had to do all his homework before going out to play with his friends. He was not a "happy camper" and the next marking period showed not only no improvement in grades, but his attention in class had gone down a grade. Aunt Bee, who lived with them, asked Andy if he was really using the right approach. After first defending his position, Andy agreed that maybe a different approach was required. That afternoon when Opie came home from school, Andy suggested that they go out and throw a football. The weight on Opie's back had been lifted and things improved quickly. Stern talk to one person might be in order, but to another, understanding his motivation and age might dictate a different approach.

While heading up a research effort of about one hundred associates, a problem was brought to my attention by one of the directors. A young Ph.D., whom we had hired a year earlier with impressive recommendations, was coasting and his research output was marginal. There was worry that his attitude was detrimental to our group. A suggestion was made that we consider severing his employment. I decided that with his training and excellent references, we should first try to find out what was the problem. I called him to my office and asked how he liked the company and his peer associates. Everything was just fine according to him. I let him know of our significant expectations of what he would bring to our research effort and that we felt let down. I assured him that we had every confidence in his ability. It was his work ethic and accomplishments which were troubling. He remarked that he did not realize what we were expecting and after working hard for his Ph.D., he had eased up a little this past year.

Initially I had felt that he needed a good "kick in the pants" and a performance ultimatum. However after listening to him, I gave him a pat on the back and said let's get together in six months. I assured him that I believed that things would look better. A remarkable turnaround in performance occurred and eighteen months later, he was awarded the "Most Outstanding Research Award" for his accomplishments over the last year.

Empathy and understanding can help smooth the way for accomplishing the best final results.

The right words plus a pat beats a fight on the mat.

Chapter Twenty-Six
Words

In any negotiation of monumental importance just a few words or phrases can be powerful motivators and help dictate the results. Many years ago Jesse Jackson, a persuasive leader of the African American community, wanted to encourage his people. He enunciated a three-word phrase, "Keep Hope Alive." This was a rallying cry to help struggling blacks not to give up their hopes and dreams but keep pursuing their goals. He repeated this cry over and over and many of his followers never gave up. They were hooked and met the challenge. "Keep Hope Alive" meant better days were surely just around the corner and gave renewed strength to their hopes.

Earlier there had been a dynamic black preacher who exhorted blacks to not only hope for better days but to utilize civil disobedience against laws they felt were unjust. Sit-ins at drugstore counters which were for "whites only" became common. Finally on August 28, 1963 on the steps of the Lincoln Memorial in Washington, D.C. before a crowd of thousands and carried on major television networks, Dr. Martin Luther King, Jr., a Baptist minister, gave his most famous speech known today as "I Have a Dream." A few of his words are as follows:

> I have a dream that one day this nation will raise up and live out the true meaning of its creed: "We hold these truths to be self-evident: that all men are created equal." I have a dream that one day.... in Alabama, little black boys and black girls will be able to join hands with little white boys and white girls as sisters and brothers.

This speech not only affected blacks, but it stirred the conscience of a major section of the white community. Very soon the "silent majority" understood that our country needed a change in attitude. This speech is credited with mobilizing supporters of desegregation and aiding greatly the passing of the 1964 Civil Rights Act. In a few short years the atmosphere, relationships, and understanding between whites and blacks changed. Today we have a black president. Yes, Dr. Martin Luther King, Jr. had a dream and it is becoming a reality.

Words can also hurt one's cherished goals and ambitions. During the 2008 campaign for president of the United States, there were some negative signs on the visible horizon about the economic conditions facing our country. In mid-September John McCain, the Republican presidential candidate, tried to give a positive spin to the situation. He publicly stated that the "fundamentals of the economy are strong." Shortly after making this claim, many factors including mass labor layoffs and major company bankruptcies occurred. John McCain appeared to be out of touch with reality and his campaign for the presidency was soon in deep trouble. Many reasons can be given for his campaign losing steam, but many believe that a few poorly chosen words were a critical blow to his aspirations.

MacArthur kept his promise.
October 20, 1944

Another historical event that emphasized the importance of words occurred as the U.S. entered World War II. The Japanese had quickly captured the Philippine Islands which had been under the control of the United States. The powers in Washington ordered the general in charge of our troops to leave the major island, Luzon, and go to Australia for further orders. When he left for Australia he gave a three-word promise, "I Shall Return." This promise gave not only hope to the Philippine people, but also made a commitment for the United States. On October 20, 1944 just a little over two years after Douglas MacArthur's pledge, the U.S. invaded the island, Leyte, in the Philippines, and I took part in the D-day landing. Shortly after the beach was partially secured, several yards from our ship some of my friends saw General MacArthur come wading ashore. They said it was a moving sight. Within two days of our landing, with the Japanese still in control, I had young Philippine boys volunteer to help me with our unloading chores. MacArthur had returned and they knew it.

The right choices of words are very powerful motivators and have been decisive in the results of negotiations and events in our country's history.

Words can speak just as loud as actions.

Chapter Twenty-Seven
Negotiating for Your Future

When do you decide what occupation you want to pursue for your life's work? Some know at a very early age and want to either follow in the footsteps of one of their parents or a role model whom they admire. However, most are probably undecided until they are in high school or college. Some do not reach a decision until they are already out working. It is such an important decision that it is never too early to start giving it some serious thought.

A few things I have learned are that no matter what you originally decide, it is helpful to have a mentor and a network of people whom you admire and who know of your talents. Equally important is to have a back-up plan. The back-up plan might be very different or in many cases just a slight deviation in time or substance from your original main goal. Life has a way of throwing many different obstacles in your path, so the virtue of persistence is key.

In our family my father was a lawyer and my mother had been a schoolteacher. Neither profession interested me much, but my older brother did follow in my father's footsteps. In high school my chemistry teacher, Mr. Newe, was a gentle, bright, young man who was studying for his Ph.D. at Fordham University in the Bronx. He was working to help pay his tuition and expenses in graduate school and to obtain teaching experience. We had forty students in our chemistry class because the alternate class was to learn Greek. Only a fourth of our class was truly interested in science, and we enjoyed both the class and laboratory to the fullest extent.

Our teacher recognized the interest of our small group and was most generous with his time and gave us help and guidance. I made up my mind that year that chemistry was going to be my life's work.

My mom had died from cancer so my original goal was to work in biochemical research and if possible aid in finding a cure for this dreaded disease. After a tour in the Navy during WWII, I finished my academic career. In 1950 with my wife, my first daughter, and a newly granted Ph.D. in organic chemistry, it was time to enter the business world. Opportunities for research chemists were scarce, but I finally located a position with the Union Carbide Company in West Virginia. There were one thousand people in Research and Development (R&D) and a great opportunity to truly learn my profession. When I first arrived, the only position still available was in plastics research. Thus, my main goal took a detour in favor of supporting my family.

Four years later a position opened up in agricultural chemical/ biological research, and the company allowed me to switch my career path to one closer to my original goal. I worked in this field for the next twenty-eight years starting as a bench chemist and ending up in charge of a large research department made up of chemists, engineers and biologists.

We live in a fast changing world and many people find they have to make major career changes in order to support their family. A relative's husband, Richard, earned a Ph.D. in nuclear physics and was employed in the nuclear power engineering field. However, after the March 28, 1979 disaster at the Three Mile Island nuclear power plant in Middleton, Pennsylvania, our country halted all development of nuclear power plants. Opportunities in that field soon became scarce.

Richard was very adaptable and worked for several years in research for an engineering firm until that department was eliminated. He then went back for further training and became a computer programmer. This went well for a time until his company outsourced most of its work overseas where it could be done at a lower cost. To help ensure his children had the advantage of higher education, his wife took a position with a hospital, and Richard became a high school teacher. Their children are all college-educated and one is now a medical doctor. Richard's flexibility, determination, and persistence overcame many obstacles and led to the family's success.

An early example of negotiating future success through flexibility, determination and persistence was that of a young man born April 6, 1726 in Muro, Italy. He was so frail that he was baptized that first day. As a youngster he always felt close to God and his church. When he was twelve years old, he supported the family as an apprentice to a tailor. When he was sixteen, he made a switch and for three years assumed the position as a servant for the local Bishop of Lacedonia until the prelate died. He would do any and all tasks as he felt he was doing what God wanted him to do. He then returned to Muro and became a tailor for two years but remained poor as he gave most of his money to the underprivileged and to his church. He then decided he wanted only to serve God and applied to the Capuchin monastery at Muro. Because of his poor health, he was rejected. A short time later in 1749, when he was twenty-three years old, a group of Redemptorist missionaries came to Muro. He decided this was his best opportunity to serve God and applied to join the mission. No matter how hard he persisted, the head of the mission turned him down. Later, when the traveling mission was leaving town, the head of the mission, Father Cafaro convinced the young man's mother to lock him in his room so he could not follow them. Not to be outdone, he climbed out his window and followed the mission out of town. He convinced Father Cafaro to give him a try as a lay brother. As they say "The rest is history." He took his vows as a lay brother in 1752. Although always in poor health, his zeal, love and devotion to God and to all people in need influenced everyone. He became well known as a most spiritual and compassionate person both inside his congregation and to all the areas where he lived and traveled.

In 1755 Gerard Majella died at the age of twenty-nine. The number of miracles attributed to him both during his life and after his death are too numerous to count. A few examples while he was still alive include bringing a boy back to life after the youngster had fallen from a cliff, and another was the multiplication of bread that was being distributed to the poor.

He was canonized a saint on December 11, 1904 by Pope Pius X. There are numerous churches throughout the world which bear his name, Saint Gerard.[1]

Flexibility, determination, persistence and faith are the essentials in negotiating your future.

---

1   For more information about St. Gerard, see the Redemptorist website. http://www.cssr.com/english/saintsblessed/stmajella.shtml

Chapter Twenty-Eight
Quit, But Don't Leave

Almost everyone has had to end a relationship, whether it is with a person, social group, church, company or other association. Sometimes you have a better opportunity and hate to leave, but at other times you leave with a somewhat bitter taste in your mouth as something has gone wrong.

I was employed in chemical research for four different Fortune 500 companies before retiring and going to Florida and entering the real estate business with my wife. My biggest turmoil happened with my first company, Union Carbide. After several years as their insecticide project leader with the help of a mentor, I had learned the duties and operation of the entire agricultural pesticide group. One day my boss called me to his office and informed me that in the near future he would be taking a different position within the company and I would be promoted to head the entire agricultural synthesis program. This raised my spirits as my wife and I had recently built a new home for our growing family, and I was ready for the new challenge. However, shortly after my boss was transferred, the announcement was made that a young, relatively new chemist was being promoted to head our agricultural synthesis group. He had received his Ph.D. degree at a prestigious west coast university and had been hired a few years earlier by the then Director of Research who was now our Vice President. The announcement came as quite a shock as I had just helped develop a new major product and process and had recently finished a speaking tour for the company to enhance its introduction to the agricultural trade. My new boss quickly let me know that the specific area of research that I was working on would be terminated, and I should look for an entirely new area. This made little sense to me or some of the middle management in our research department, and I was given an immediate six-month reprieve to continue my current research program.

My wife and I discussed the situation for a few sleepless nights. We were well situated in our new house and had lots of good friends and an active social life which was focused around our church. However, with a very limited business future it was time to examine new opportunities. It didn't take but a few months, and I was offered a new position where I would have the opportunity to head up a small agricultural research program.

My last two months at Union Carbide were difficult. I felt betrayed by senior management, and I also believed that the new head of the pesticide synthesis group had little pertinent experience and a very different vision for the program.

One bright light in my leaving was the attitude of two of the assistant directors who appreciated the work that I had been doing. They wished me well and seemed positive about my future. Even though I felt bitter towards top management, I decided to burn no bridges. I did not discuss my personal feelings with anyone except my wife. I let all my fellow workers know how much I would miss them and thanked them for all their cooperation.

Ten years later the company I was then working for, Esso Chemical, made the decision to abandon their effort in the agricultural field. Esso had treated me extremely well and had recently placed me in their bonus pool for work that I had accomplished. They also promised me a position in a different department. However, based on a recommendation to a headhunter by one of the assistant directors of my first company, Union Carbide, I was offered and accepted the position of Vice President of Research of The Scotts Company, a leading lawn and garden company. Leaving that first company with all bridges still intact proved to have been the best decision I could have made.

I firmly believe –

When you take your final walk under the exit sign, never slam the door.

Chapter Twenty-Nine
The Letter

Betts, the love of my life

In early 1945 my LST ship had recently participated in the invasion of Luzon, an island in the Philippines, and we were awaiting new orders. We had picked up a new captain and were in a training mode as a third of the crew had been replaced. Mail call was rare in the areas where we had been lately so when bags of mail were brought on board, excitement ran high. It was then that I received *The Letter*. It started as usual Dear John, but quickly took on the mantle of the often despised "Dear John" letters. My gal, Betts, the love of my life, explained that she had met a Marine and they were quite fond of each other. She gave me his name and the rest of the letter was just a gentle good-bye. I was devastated as I had never met another girl in my life that had captured my every desire. I had never thought that we would ever part.

I then realized that I had written very few letters to her in the past year. In view of the fact that we were seldom in any area to send or receive mail, I only wrote once a month or so and then my thoughts were about the tasks just accomplished and what lay ahead. In truth, they were not the warm letters that should have been written by a guy to his only love. I showed her letter to my bunkmate, the engineering officer. He was about my age and gave me good moral support. I wrote to Betts and remembered saying, "I could not stop loving her all at once." The rest was an apology for not writing more often and expressing my true feelings about how much she meant to me.

The Good Lord must have heard my prayers for we shortly received orders to return to the States instead of participating in the next invasion which was Okinawa. As soon as we landed in San Diego, I quickly got thirty dollars in quarters, went to the nearest pay phone, and talked to Betts until my money ran out. I immediately sent off a letter to reinforce my feelings towards her, and just hoped she felt the same towards me.

After about four anxious weeks it was my turn for a month's leave. As soon as I arrived home, I called Betts. She seemed as happy as I was anxious, and we met within the hour. As soon as we saw each other, we both ran into each others arms and we knew it was forever. We became engaged that night, and we were married the following year after a short, second overseas tour.

I learned that when any negotiation or relationship starts to slip away, first examine where YOU made mistakes. If you correct them quickly, then you can expect the truth of the saying-

"All's well that ends well."

Chapter Thirty
The Great Negotiator

Many people have wanted something so very much that they promised God that if it happened, they would do something special in return. I have been a member of that group for a long time. It is also very interesting that what we hope for and what we receive are not always the same, but most often what we receive is better. In Chapter 28, I discussed how I did not receive a promotion that had been promised. I believe that my wife and I prayed fervently that the promotion would happen. We thought that I had not only earned the promotion but also the salary increase that went with it.

Over the next few years the outcome of not obtaining that promotion made it clear to me that the Great Negotiator not only listens but is truly looking out for us. The relatively young, new Ph.D. who had been made head of the pesticide group lasted for only about two years. There were some problems, and he left the company to pursue an academic career. An experienced chemist who was close to the pesticide program was put in charge of the group. A young chemist who had taken over my position as the insecticide project leader was also doing very well. However, disaster struck. There was a major meeting in Saint Louis of several units of the agricultural program including research, development, and sales. The plane carrying the chemical research group crashed and all were killed. This included the group leader and the insecticide project leader. I could have held either of those two positions. The Great Negotiator had His own reasons why I was denied that promotion a few years earlier, and I decided to leave the company.

In early 1944 I was an ensign in the Navy assigned to an LST amphibious vessel. We were docked in New Orleans and not scheduled to leave for the Pacific for a few weeks. I was twenty years old and had fallen in love with a very special, young lady. We had met about a year and a half earlier, but my naval duties and her being far away at college had limited us to only a few weeks of courtship.

In any major city such as New Orleans with so many men away in the service, a young naval officer had no trouble getting dates. However, there was only one date I really wanted. I promised the Lord that I would have absolutely no dates in New Orleans if He would let me see my gal, Betts, just once more before I left for overseas. I asked our captain for a few days leave as I had not had any leave since I had received my commission about six months earlier. The captain would not grant even a short, one-week leave to anyone. Instead he granted overnight liberty to half of the crew each day. Thus, my hope to see Betts at that time was not possible. However, I kept my pledge to the Lord and did not date anyone in New Orleans.

About a year later after serving in two invasions in the Philippines, the events of the chapter, *The Letter*, took place. Thus, instead of receiving a few days leave before shipping out in New Orleans, The Great Negotiator arranged to get me home at a much more opportune time. My wife and I had sixty-one years of loving, devoted life together. In just these two negotiations, the Great Negotiator saved my LIFE and gave me my WIFE and ultimately six wonderful daughters. Who could ask for more?

With the Great Negotiator, you don't always get what you want but you get what you need.

www.ingramcontent.com/pod-product-compliance
Lightning Source LLC
Chambersburg PA
CBHW030402290526
45785CB00004B/1868